SAYINGS OF THE
Buddha
Reflections for Every Day

William Wray

Capella

This edition published in 2007 by
Arcturus Publishing Limited
26/27 Bickels Yard, 151–153 Bermondsey Street,
London SE1 3HA

ISBN: 978-1-84193-578-2

Printed in Singapore

Contents

Introduction

Buddhism is considered to be one of the most important world faiths and it certainly has its influence on the spiritual life of the planet. It is estimated that half the countries of the world have been directly influenced by Buddhist thinking. How many practising Buddhists actually exist on the face of the globe is hard to estimate, but what is evident is that the power of Buddhism to capture the imagination of the human mind is as strong today as it was when the Buddha gave his doctrine of 'The Middle Way' to a gathering of five men who had been his original followers in the Deer Park in Saranath in about 450 BC.

This was a teaching that he himself thought long and hard about before delivering because he thought it so subtle and demanding that few would be able to follow, and yet, here in a time in which materialism is said to govern our thinking, the power of this man's spiritual realization still has a profound influence, and a growing one, particularly as far as the West is concerned. This says a lot about what this one man discovered in deep meditation. It also says a lot about us as human beings. Are his words of such forceful influence because they speak directly to something which all of us hold within us and in our more penetrating moments dimly realize?

An answer to this question can only be discovered if we devote time to a consideration of what he realized in his own life and sought to express in the years he spent teaching.

Arranged in the form of daily reflections, this book contains a range of aphorisms which express in different ways the core doctrines of Buddhism. They are derived mainly from the Pali Canon, written in the first century BC. This is a collection of manuscripts which recorded in writing the words of the Buddha that had previously been passed on orally. Also contained in the book are extracts of other works which hold a central position in the vast outpouring of the human spirit which constitutes Buddhist literature.

Life of the Buddha

So what do we know about this man called the 'Buddha'? The first thing we have to realize is that this is not so much a name as an indication of his state of being. The Buddha is a title given to somebody of the highest spiritual understanding. It means 'One Who is Awake'. He is awake not in the way that we normally understand being awake. We are awake only to a dream of life within which we seek to create an identity. What this man was awake to was spiritual reality, things as they are in truth.

His name was Siddhartha Gautama. He was born in 487 BC in Lumbini, a state that spanned the border of modern-day Nepal and Northern India. He was born into the Kshatriya, the warrior caste, part of a ruling family. His father was determined to provide for his son: legend has it that Siddhartha was raised in a palace surrounded by high walls to prevent him from witnessing the suffering that is part of human experience.

His mother had a dream on conception that a white baby elephant entered her side. From this the seers predicted that Siddhartha would one day be either a great political or religious leader. We can only speculate as to whether or not his father was trying to shield him from the pain and suffering that can easily be central to the human lot. This seems likely, especially given that Siddhartha's own mother died when he was only seven days old. Another possibility is that in the light of the seers' prediction his father was concerned that one day Siddhartha would give up his privileged life and seek spiritual enlightenment as a way of transcending the sorrows of this world. Whatever the reason for his action, at the age of 29 Siddhartha slipped away in the night to become a wandering monk.

Before this Siddhartha had been raised with all the advantages his status in society was able to provide. At the age of 16 he was married to the beautiful Yahodra who bore him a son, Rahula. Despite the luxury of his life, this intelligent and sensitive man felt a lack; there was a spiritual understanding that wasn't available to him.

Later legend states that all of this came to a climax with four journeys he took out of the palace. On the first one of these, his father, determined to protect his son, arranged for the streets to be filled with happy and healthy people. He had all the old and infirm removed from view, but as chance would have it one remained undetected. When Siddhartha saw this, he commanded his charioteer to return to the palace in order to reflect upon what it meant to grow old. In his second journey he encountered a sick man and on the third a funeral procession. All this inevitably led him to ponder upon the transient nature of human existence, which no amount of privilege could protect him from. On his fourth journey he spoke to a holy man, a conversation which sowed in him the belief that it was possible to find a spiritual solution to what today we call existential misery.

Whether this legend is true or not, what is evident is that what he was facing in his life were the questions which we have all considered in some way. How do we find fulfilment in life?

How do we overcome the pain that can so easily be our lot?

What is the meaning of human existence and how might we discover the Truth? For Siddhartha, these questions were so pressing that he stole away in the middle of the night, left his family, his wife and child and renounced the world.

Wandering monks who had turned their back on worldly life were a familiar part of Indian life, as they are to this very day, in a land where schools of philosophy and gurus of various kinds abound. Siddhartha's first teacher, Ajara Kalama, taught him meditational techniques which encouraged ever deeper insight. His nature was such that he quickly mastered the techniques and achieved what was known as 'the sphere of nothingness'. Although such techniques granted more than a touch of bliss, the pain and suffering he encountered in the world as we know it remained regardless of the ease of mind discovered during meditation.

Siddhartha went on to study under Uddaka Ramaputta, who taught him techniques which allowed him to enter ever finer states, including the one described as 'the sphere of neither perception nor non-perception'. He recognized the validity of these states, but he also realized, sublime as they were, they were not what he was seeking.

After this he turned to austerity as a means of discovering that which he sought. He first developed breath control techniques which were based on reducing the intake of air, so much so that in practising these techniques it became possible to hardly breathe at all.

He then began reducing his intake of food. He carried this through until he was existing on one spoon of bean soup a day. For six years he practised these austerities, determined that through them he would achieve the enlightenment which he was seeking. What he discovered instead was that a life of extreme asceticism not only took its inevitable toll on his body but gave him nothing of what he was questing after. He came to the conclusion that rather than pursuing these extreme attempts to achieve realization, the only solution was to adopt what he came to describe as the 'Middle Way', neither over-indulgence nor self-mortification.

When he had come to this conclusion the small band of fol-lowers who had attached themselves to him over the years felt that he had turned his back on the path upon which they were depending upon him to lead them, and deserted him.

He was left to himself with no one to support him, his family gone, his followers gone, his reputation as man of insight and understanding ruined. Entirely alone, he was determined on one thing, the goal that he had always set himself: to cut through the maya, the veil of ignorance, and discover life's cen-tral reality, the source of true understanding.

It was at this point that a childhood memory came to mind. It was of his father ploughing whilst Siddhartha sat in the shade of a rose-apple tree. The steady measure of the ox-team, the play of sunlight and shade had allowed him so easily to slip below the surface of life and discover, unlooked for, what he now so desperately sought. Was 'Enlightenment' easy, so natu-ral to man that it was child's play? Was he in all his desperate determination missing out on what was immediately to hand?

As this thought arose, he made up his mind that regardless of what was granted him, he would not take another step in this life until he found what he sought. He sat beneath a large, spreading tree and entered into meditation. In the course of one night he achieved the goal he had set himself, spiritual awakening. Having overcome the force of worldly temptation, he, through contemplation, obtained knowledge of the contin-ual cycle of lives, not only those that he had encountered personally but also the lives of all as they rose and fell. He saw how people forged their own lives, of how they were subject to their own actions. He saw the direct link between craving and suffering. He saw his own identity dissolve into the totality of being, the source of true understanding. In the final watch of the night he attained full enlightenment. It was at this point that Siddhartha Gautama became the Buddha. He awoke from the dream of life and became enlightened.

For seven weeks he remained, reflecting on what had been revealed to him, wondering if there was any possibility that the insight he had been granted could ever be communicated. His first thought was that he should remain in seclusion, but the compassion for which the Buddha became renowned dictated that he should return to the world, to teach and devote the rest of his life to 'Turning the Wheel of the Law'. He walked the hundred miles to Saranath, seeking the five men who had deserted him. If they could be made to understand, there was the chance that others might be made to understand as well. He found them in the Deer Park in Saranath.

When they saw him their first response was to reject him. They were determined on a path of extreme asceticism, and they saw only what they considered to be his weakness. Even so there was something about this man that was undeniably powerful, and despite themselves they entered into a debate. Slowly they began to understand. They began to see what he had seen. Over days, not only by the power of his teaching, but also by the power of his presence, one by one, he led them to a state of Enlightenment.

From this he knew that others could also be led to understanding, and having made a spiritual journey he commenced a physical one, a journey which would last for forty-five years, during which time he wandered from place to place teaching, his brotherhood, or sangha, growing and growing, with more and more men and women coming to achieve what he had achieved. Buddhism speaks of what can be understood and known when there is a determination to go beyond the world as it is usually experienced, when there is a determination to arise out of the sleep of life and achieve what the Buddha described as Nirvana.

His Teaching

So what were the truths that the Buddha managed to convince his first five followers of in the Deer Park? At the heart of this discourse were what became known as the Four Noble Truths. These take the form of a formal medical diagnosis as to the mass of ill that is associated with life. As with all medical assessment it consists of diagnosis and treatment. Life is suffering. Suffering is caused by craving. There can be an end to suffering. There is a way that leads to the end of suffering.

The first of these Truths explores how life has about it an essential suffering, not only the obvious suffering caused by disease and death, but also the suffering caused by loss: the loss of one's loved ones, the loss of those things that one holds dear. It pointed out that even when one is in possession of something there is the fear of loss. We strive and strain to get what we want and then fear to lose. All this involves suffering.

What the Buddha claims is that the five elements that constitute the individual all have inherent within them the element of suffering.

The five elements to which he refers are the physical body, sensation and feeling, cognition, individual characteristics and consciousness.

Clearly what is being referred to here are the constituent elements which go to make this so-called individual. To the Buddha all of these are not so much a hierarchy of elements, more a series of dependencies, none of which can stand by itself alone. Every part is reliant on every other part rather than gathered round a personal identity, or soul. There is nothing left to cling to as some kind of separate self. With a conclusion of this kind the individual is forced to give way. It is in fact blown away, and this is the literal meaning of the word nirvana.

The second of the four Noble Truths identifies the source of suffering as craving. The first of these cravings is the strong desire for all that is pleasant in life, the thirst for sensual satisfaction, with the mind constantly fixed on achieving ways of gaining that satisfaction. The second craving is for life itself, the desire to cling on and possess. The third is the opposite, the desire to reject, revile and finally to destroy. This desire can at best take the form of aversion to those things that we find unpleasant, at worst to an entirely destructive attitude to life out of which arises a whole range of criticism, and general negativity. Inevitably there is something that lies at the heart of all this desire and aversion, a forceful sense of self-identification, the ego and all its conflicting demands.

The Third Noble Truth makes it quite clear that there is a cure from this mass of suffering, and that cure is the direct result of the ending of craving by renouncing it, rejecting it, by non-attachment to it. When the bond is broken, freedom arises. This is clearly a path of self-abnegation, and it is the little self, the realm of me and mine, that according to the Buddha's course of treatment needs to be dissolved. This act of dissolution is nirvana. As his was not a philosophy of attainment – in fact the attempt to try and seize something as a personal possession, does nothing, according to the Buddha, but reinforce the separate self – he would not be drawn as to what lay beyond, but the blissful expression on the face of countless images of the meditating Buddha gives an indication of what occurs when the confines of the heart and mind give way. What are these confines? The Buddha said they were greed, hatred and delusion. When these are dissolved then the truth is revealed, love is revealed and generosity of spirit is revealed. These are not to be sought for and grasped by some imaginary individual. They naturally arise when this little self is laid down.

Within the Fourth Noble Truth is an outline of the treatment prescribed by the Buddha to bring about the end of suffering. This treatment involves the development of the following: Right View, Right Resolve, Right Speech, Right Action, Right Livelihood, Right Effort, Right Mindfulness, Right Meditation. All of this constitutes the Middle Way, the path in life in which the extremes of excessive indulgence and excessive austerity are avoided. This is the path that leads out of delusion towards the truth. The word 'path' suggests a journey, and here are contained a series of recommended actions which will allow that journey to be made. As has already been stated, the Buddha was more interested in practice than metaphysical speculation, and what is listed here are practical measures which if employed have an utterly transformative effect. They are measures that should be adopted by those who wish to free themselves from the cycle of samsara, the cycle of life and death.

Although the Buddha taught that there is, in the final analysis, no individual identity as such, those things to which we devote ourselves have a karmic effect on future lives which arise 'like one fire lit from another'.

When looking at the Eightfold Path it becomes evident that the eight may be divided into three distinct areas of life, areas that were of particular concern to the Buddha. These are wisdom, morality and meditation.

Wisdom involves Right View or coming to a proper understanding of the truth of the Buddha's teaching. All of us have had an insight, a flash of understanding, when our view suddenly changes. With that flash arises the realization that life as we know it has its limitations. In moments of greater awareness the sense of separation normally experienced gives way to a deep appreciation of the underlying unity, a unity from which we are in no way separate. From this experience there may arise a resolution to come to a deeper and more lasting understanding of the true nature of things. This is Right Resolve, and as part of this resolution there may arise the steady determination to meet and counter those deep ingrained habits of heart and mind that force us into a state of separation and suffering. Involving both heart and mind, the decision to be made is both emotional and intellectual. This is the second aspect of wisdom.

Morality involves speech, action and the way we gain our livelihood. Right Speech concerns the truth, holding the words of truth in mind, and speaking from that truth in a way that is true. This doesn't mean that these words remain as a set of ideas which we as individuals have identified with and tried to claim. These are the words of truth discovered in experience and spoken in a way that causes no harm.

Words are all important. Our experience of the world is forged out of the ideas that we carry with us. If we avoid not only lying to others but also lying to ourselves, everything will not only be freed from the distortions we have imposed but will become purified and therefore more translucent and luminous.

Right Action is a direct result of refined ideas. If our words are of the nature of greed, hatred and delusion then must our action be likewise. How different are actions that arise out of their opposites: generosity, compassion and understanding. These are skilful actions which are quite different from the clumsy results of egotistical prompting. Actions such as these, because of the limits placed upon them by the nature of their source, are bound to be mistimed and mis-measured, and rather than unify and resolve, will inevitably create division. Skilful actions, which draw together and break down division, come from an altogether different source and have an altogether different quality.

Right Livelihood encourages us to seek a way of sustaining ourselves which minimizes the impact we have on others and the world in general. In gaining our living we may feel that circumstances force us into ignoring such considerations, but Right Livelihood encourages us to think differently, to appreciate the interconnectedness of all things and to tread lightly with due care and compassion.

The third main area dealt with in the Eightfold Path is meditation. This is not surprising given that Siddhartha became the Buddha through single pointed meditation. He resolved to attain Enlightenment. He sat upon the ground and swore that 'Flesh may wither, blood may dry up, but I shall not leave this seat until I gain Enlightenment!' Such resolution is therefore an essential part of the meditative process, to remain undeflected and undeterred regardless of the difficulties encountered. Inevitably there are mental traits, deep ingrained habits of heart and mind which need to be countered with steady determination.

Right Mindfulness is one of the great joys of the reflective life. When we adopt mindfulness we immediately allow for quiet observation; the possibility that, rather than being utterly identified with all the thoughts and feelings which rise in the heart and mind, we have the capacity to stand back and quietly observe the promptings of self-identification. What Mindfulness also does is draw us out of all the concerns for the past and future, all the confusion that arises out of a self-created imaginary world, and to bring us back to the immediate reality of the here and now. To be dominated by thoughts and feelings which are in a state of constant flux is not a way of bringing steadiness and consistency to our actions. The movements of the mind are many; the unidentified observer is unitary, therefore, calm and clear.

Calmness and clarity are much desired, but personal desire will never provide them. Desire has the opposite effect. It agitates rather than calms. It confuses rather than clarifies. But as has already been stated, quiet determination is another thing. It involves laying aside all wishes for oneself, giving up this little self and recognising it for what it is, a matrix of elements. It is not therefore some kind of personal attainment that is being sought in meditation, but rather a dissolution of all that holds us confined. Remember the Buddha's own experience watching his father ploughing whilst he sat in the shade of a rose-apple tree, of how he quite naturally slipped below the surface of life and discovered 'Enlightenment'. It is about dissolving and merging, the key ingredients of the reflective life. And it is reflection that is being offered by this book, words to be carried into daily life, to be held in mind as an oasis of peace and bliss.

Although the daily reflections which follow are drawn primarily from the Pali Texts which formed the original corpus of Buddhist thinking, even those that are not are much respected and therefore in accord with the Buddha's original teaching. The very fact that the texts have been chosen for reflection is very much in keeping with the Buddha's avowed purpose, not speculation but transformation. As has already been stressed, Buddhism is a practical philosophy. These texts are for a practical purpose.

To reflect upon the words of the Buddha, to allow them to suffuse the heart and mind is a time-honoured way of coming to a true understanding of what is meant. This is not theoretical understanding – yet more ideas to add to the general stock of information we already possess. Reflecting upon these texts will allow there to arise a deeper understanding of how to live in harmony and not discord, in unity and not division, in Truth and not delusion.

Carry the book with you or write down the day's thought for continual reference. Many of these texts were learnt by heart and passed on from generation to generation. Why not follow suit and learn some of them by heart, especially those that have a particular resonance? Rather than making up your mind as to their meaning, hold them in mind and allow their significance to have its effect on the way you experience life.

January

DAILY REFLECTIONS

January 1

**Truth is one.
There is no second.**

January 2

May all be happy and
at their ease!
May they be joyous and
live in safety!

January 3

So I went forth from home in the houseless state, a quester of what is good, seeking the incomparable path to peace.

January 4

Just as a lotus, blue, red or white,
though born in the water, grown up
in the water, when it reaches the
surface stands there unsoiled by the
water – just so, though born in the
world, grown up in the world,
having overcome the world,
I abide unsoiled by the world.
Take it that I am awake.

January 5

Standing or walking,
sitting or lying down, during
all these waking hours, let him
establish mindfulness of good will,
which men call the highest state!

January 6

'When you spoke of wholesome
dharmas which ones did you mean?'
'I meant morality, faith, vigour,
mindfulness and concentration.'

January 7

Watchful amongst the unwatchful,
awake amongst those that sleep,
the wise man like a swift horse runs
his race, outrunning those
who are slow.

January 8

I have seen an ancient way,
an ancient road followed by the
wholly awakened ones of old.
Along that I have gone and things
that I have I come to know have I
passed on to you, this Brahma-faring
that is prosperous and flourishing,
widespread and widely known.

January 9

What we are today comes
from our thoughts of yesterday,
and present thoughts build
our life of tomorrow: our life is the
creation of our mind.

January 10

He, having obtained mastery
of self, abandons wrong, makes
right become, abandons what is
blameworthy, makes what is
blameless become; he guards
the pure Self. This is called
mastery of self.

January 11

Gautama lives as one who has
laid aside the club and sword.
He is scrupulous, kindly, friendly
and compassionate towards all
breathing things.

January 12

As a builder of a city when constructing a town first of all clears the site, removes all stumps and thorns, and levels it; and only after that he lays out and marks off the roads and cross-roads, and so builds the city, even so the Yogin develops the five cardinal virtues with morality as his support, with morality as his basis.

January 13

Abandoning harsh speech, the recluse Gautama abstains from it. Whatever speech is gentle, pleasing to the ear, affectionate, going to the heart, urbane, pleasant and agreeable, such is his speech.

January 14

If a man speaks or acts with an impure mind, suffering follows him as the wheel of the cart follows the beast that draws it.

January 15

He who for the sake of
happiness hurts others who
also want happiness, shall not
hereafter find happiness.

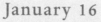

January 16

When faith arises it arrests
the Five Hindrances and the heart
becomes free from them, clear,
serene and undisturbed.

January 17

Never speak harsh words, for once
spoken they may return to you.
Angry words are painful and there
may be blows for blows.

January 18

To neglect the highest
dharma, and instead to
think demeritorious thoughts,
is like neglecting the jewels on
the jewel-island and collecting
lumps of earth instead.

January 19

Abandoning what is unwholesome, you ought to ponder what is wholesome, for that will bring you advantages in this world and help you to win the highest goal.

January 20

An artist once a picture painted
of such a monster that he fainted.
So endlessly worlds transmigrate
by false ideas infatuate.

January 21

As stars, a fault of vision,
as a lamp,
a mock show, dew-drops
or a bubble,
a dream, a lightning flash,
or cloud,
so should we view what
is conditioned.

January 22

There will come a time when the name of this hill will vanish, and these people will pass away and I will attain utter nirvana.

January 23

When the recluse speaks much,
'tis of and on the goal;
knowing of dharma tells,
knowing he speaketh much.

January 24

When wisdom arises it dispels
the darkness of ignorance,
generates the illumination
of knowledge, sheds the light
of cognition and makes holy
truths stand out clearly.

January 25

If material shape is impermanent,
and if that which impermanent is
suffering, you cannot regard that
which is impermanent, suffering and
liable to change as: This is mine, I
am this, this is my Self.

January 26

The wise do not take delight in
the senses and their objects,
are not impressed by them,
are not attached to them and
in consequence their craving ceases.

January 27

If a man speaks or acts with
a pure mind, joy follows him
as his own shadow.

January 28

Hate is not conquered by hate:
hate is conquered by love.
This is a law eternal.

January 29

This contemplation is one
which I, mindful, enter upon and
mindful emerge from.

January 30

The cessation of craving
successively leads to that of
grasping, of becoming, of birth,
of old age and death,
of grief, lamentation, pain,
sadness and despair.

January 31

Many do not know that we are here in this world to live in harmony. Those who know this do not fight against each other.

February

DAILY REFLECTIONS

February 1

As a mountain peak is free
from all desire to please or
displease, so is nirvana.

February 2

I call him man-of-calm;
no heeding lusts.
Without a knot, he hath the
foul mire crossed.

February 3

And those in high thought and in deep contemplation, with ever-living power advance on the path, they in the end find nirvana, the peace supreme and infinite joy.

February 4

Happy indeed are the men-of-worth,
in them no craving's seen.
The 'I' conceit is rooted up;
delusion's net is burst.

February 5

By arising in faith and watchfulness,
by self-reflection and self-harmony,
the wise man makes an island for
his soul which many waters
cannot overflow.

February 6

As the lotus is unstained by water,
so is nirvana unstained
by the defilements.

February 7

Who passion and hate and
ignorance have left,
him they call one who has made
the self become,
who is Brahma-become,
truth finder,
an awakened one, who's passed by
fear and dread,
one who has abandoned
everything.

February 8

For whatever a man thinks about
continually, to that his mind
becomes inclined by
force of habit.

February 9

The sense pleasures are not worth
paying any attention to, for they are
unreal, hollow, and uncertain,
and the happiness they give is
merely imaginary.

February 10

Warded in act and word,
in eating temperate,
with truth I clear the weeds;
and full of bliss is my deliverance.

February 11

Men who are foolish and ignorant
are careless and never watchful;
but the man who lives in
watchfulness considers it
his greatest treasure.

February 12

This through many toils I've won – Enough!
Why should I make it known?
By folk with lust and hate consumed
not this dharma that's understood.
Leading on against the stream,
deep, subtle, difficult, delicate,
unseen 'twill be by passion's slaves
cloaked in the murk of ignorance.

February 13

This dharma I teach is deep,
difficult to see, difficult to
understand, peaceful,
excellent, beyond dialectic,
subtle, intelligible to the wise.

February 14

As cool water allays feverish heat,
so also nirvana removes the craving
for sensuous enjoyments, the
craving for further becoming, the
cessation of becoming.

February 15

The royal chariots wear out,
and so too the body ages.
The true dharma does not age.

February 16

So the self-quickened, lore-adept
listener imperturbable,
by knowledge may help others muse,
the eager-eared adventurers.

February 17

Never surrender to carelessness;
never sink into weak pleasures
and lust. Those who are watchful,
in deep contemplation, reach
the end, the joy supreme.

February 18

A brightly shining fire,
when not stirred by the wind, is
soon appeased; so the unstimulated
heart of those who live in seclusion
wins peace without much effort.

February 19

Hidden in the mystery of
consciousness, the mind,
incorporeal, flies alone far away.
Those who set their mind on
harmony become free from
the bonds of death.

February 20

A person who is neither
tempter of self nor a tormentor
of others is, in this very life,
stilled, attained to nirvana,
become cool; he is one who
experiences bliss; he lives with
a self that has become Brahma.

February 21

It is no easier to deny the urges of a man who has not seen the real truth, and who finds himself standing in the fairground of the sensory world, fascinated by its brightness, than it is to deny those of a bull who is eating corn in the middle of a cornfield.

February 22

An enemy can hurt an enemy,
and a man who hates can harm
another man; but a man's own
mind, if wrongly directed, can do
him a far greater harm.

February 23

Loss of mindfulness is why people
engage in useless pursuits, do not
care for their own interests and
remain unalarmed in the presence
of things which actually menace
their welfare.

February 24

Dharma, I say, is the charioteer.

February 25

By the All-awakened One,
foreknowing, thoroughly
knowing every world, opened
is the door of the deathless;
when nirvana has been reached
there is security.

February 26

These are the ten qualities
nirvana shares with space. Neither is
born, grows old, dies, passes away, or
is reborn; both are unconquerable,
cannot be stolen, are unsupported,
are unobstructed and infinite.

February 27

Pure-limbed, white-canopied,
one-wheeled, the cart roles on.
See him that cometh: faultless,
stream-cutter, bondless he.

February 28

As a mountain peak is inaccessible, so is nirvana inaccessible to all passions. As no seed can grow on a mountain peak, so the seeds of all the passions cannot grow in nirvana.

February 29

By deeds is one a Brahmana.

March

DAILY REFLECTIONS

March 1

The mind is wavering and restless, difficult to guard and restrain. Let the wise man straighten his mind as a maker of arrows makes his arrow straight.

March 2

A mind which is not protected by mindfulness is as helpless as a blind man walking over uneven ground without a guide.

March 3

Whatever streams flow
in the world,
Ajita (said the Master then),
the dam for them
is mindfulness;
it is the floodgate too I
say; by wisdom may the
streams be closed.

March 4

Who shall conquer this world and
the world of the gods, and also the
world of Yama, of death and of
pain? Who shall find the
Dhammapada, the clear Path of
Perfection, even as a man
seeks flowers finds the
most beautiful flower?

March 5

As the bee takes the essence of a
flower and flies away without
destroying its beauty and perfume,
so let the sage wander in this life.

March 6

The holy disciple who has followed the right road sees nirvana with a mind which is pure, sublime, straight, unimpeded and disinterested.

March 7

In whom no craving spreads,
in the monk who cuts the stream,
rid of all toils and tasks,
no fret is found or known.

March 8

The wind doesn't lend itself to being grasped by the hands or to being touched. But never the less there is such a thing as wind. Just so there is nirvana but one cannot point to nirvana, either by its colour or shape.

March 9

For those following the
stream of becoming,
who are overcome by touches?
Proceeding by the false way,
distant is the destruction
of the fetters.

March 10

The perfume of the flowers goes not
against the wind, not even the
perfume of sandalwood, of rosebay,
or of jasmine; but the perfume of
virtue travels against wind and
reaches unto the ends of the world.

March 11

Streams which in the world flow
into the great ocean, and those
showers from the sky which fall into
it – yet is neither the emptiness nor
the fullness of the great ocean
affected by that.

March 12

It is not death; it is not life I cherish.
I bide my time, a servant waiting for
his wage. It is not death; it is not
life I cherish. I bide my time in
mindfulness and wisdom steeped.

March 13

If a fool can see his own folly,
he in this at least is wise; but
the fool who thinks he is wise,
he indeed is the real fool.

March 14

A wise man who wants to be saved from great danger would not want to go to sleep while ignoring his faults, which are like vicious snakes that have crept into the house.

March 15

Him the unprovokable,
him the unclouded mind,
freed of all lustfulness,
void of all indolence,
guide of those on the brink,
is master of birth-and-death.

March 16

'These are my sons.
This is my wealth.'
In this way the fool troubles himself.
He is not the owner of himself: how
much less of his sons and his wealth!

March 17

The man plunges in the spate,
flooding and turgid swift of flow,
he, borne along the current's way,
how can he others help to cross?

March 18

People are tied down by a sense
object when they cover it with
unreal imaginations; likewise
they are liberated when they
see it as it really is.

March 19

The wrong action seems sweet
to the fool until the reaction comes
and brings pain, and the bitter fruits
of wrong deeds have then to be
eaten by the fool.

104

March 20

Arise (from sloth), sir (meditating);
train swiftly for tranquility.
Let not death's king find you proud,
nor dupe you to subjection.

March 21

Slothfulness is dust...
Being prone to it is dust:
by diligence, by knowledge,
draw out the barb of self.

March 22

And if to his own harm the fool increases in cleverness, this only destroys his own mind, and his fate is worse than before.

March 23

Spotless, unobstructed, silent,
like the vast expanse of space;
who in truth does really see Thee?
The Tathagata perceives.

March 24

Faith is the seed, austerity the rain,
wisdom my yoke and plough;
my pole is modesty;
my mind is the strap
and I have mindfulness
for share and goad.

March 25

Look upon the man who tells thee thy faults as if he told thee of hidden treasure, the wise man who shows thee the dangers of life. Follow that man: he who follows him will see good and not evil.

March 26

As the drops of dew in contact
with the sun's rays disappear,
so all theorizings vanish
once one has obtained Thee.

March 27

All the great rivers on reaching the great ocean lose their former names and identities and are reckoned simply as the great ocean.

March 28

Not from anywhere Thou comest,
and to nowhere dost thou go;
in no dwelling place have the sages
ever apprehended Thee.

March 29

Who here in faith, in
moral habit grows,
in wisdom, in giving up
and in the heard,
such as she, a disciple
of moral habit,
here wins what is the
essence of the self.

March 30

Not through what is low comes the
attainment of the highest, but
through what is high comes the
attainment of the highest.

March 31

Have not for friends those whose soul is ugly; go not with men who have an evil soul. Have for friends those whose soul is beautiful; go with men whose soul is good.

April

DAILY REFLECTIONS

April 1

If your sense-organs are calm,
so will the acts of the body become
calm, calm the acts of speech,
calm the acts of mind; and one
may think: 'We will offer an
offering – calm itself – to our
fellow Brahma-farers.'

April 2

Who is able here to praise Thee,
lacking signs and featureless?
Thou the range of speech transcending,
not supported anywhere.

April 3

Awaken ye to the doctrine, exert skill,
lead the Brahma-faring, for 'there is
no immortality of anything born.'

April 4

In whatever person malice is
engendered, in that person love
should be made to become,
also compassion, also balance.

April 5

Learn this from the river's flow
in mountain cleft and chasm:
loud gush the rivulets,
the great stream silent moves.
Loud booms the empty thing.
The full is ever calm;
like pot half-full the fool,
like full pot the sage.

April 6

Who knows and curbed-of-self,
tho' knowing, speaks not much:
the sage and wisdom worths,
that sage still wisdom wins.

April 7

Just as a flower which seems beautiful and has colour but has no perfume, so are the fruitless words of the man who speaks them but does them not.

April 8

As all plants and animals which increase and grow and prosper, do so with the earth as their support, with the earth as their basis, just so the Yogin, with morality as his support, with morality as his basis, develops the five cardinal virtues: faith, vigour, mindfulness, concentration and wisdom.

April 9

When invaded by painful feeling, the
Arahat firmly grasps at the idea of
impermanence, and ties his thoughts
to the post of contemplation.

April 10

Death carries away the man who gathers the flowers of sensuous passions, even as a torrent of rushing waters overflows a sleeping village, and then runs forward on its way.

April 11

From the utter fading away
and stopping of ignorance the
constructions stop, and so stops each
of the rest. Such is the stopping of
this entire mass of ill.

April 12

Joy is born in one who has delight, the body of one who has joy is calmed, one whose body is calmed feels ease, and the mind of one who is at ease is contemplative.

April 13

Wherefore stir up energy for the attainment of the unattained, for the mastery of the unmastered, for the realization of the unrealized.
Thus will your going forth become a barren but fruitful and growing thing.

April 14

Make the Self your refuge and your lamp.

April 15

Secluded meditation guards him who meditates, lengthens his life, gives him strength and shuts out faults.

April 16

To what end should the thought:
'I am the result of my own deeds,
heir to deeds, having deeds for
matrix, deeds for kin; to me the deeds
come home again; whatever deed I
do, whether good or evil, I shall
become its heir,' be contemplated
often by man or woman?

April 17

Overcome anger by peacefulness:
overcome evil by good.
Overcome the mean by generosity;
and the man who lies by truth.

April 18

The Brahma-faring is lived for the advantage of the training, for the further wisdom, for the essence of freedom, for mastery in mindfulness.

April 19

Those who are forever watchful,
who study themselves day and night,
and who wholly strive for nirvana,
all their passions pass away.

April 20

The Great Way is calm
and large hearted,
for it nothing is easy,
nothing hard.

April 21

Those who have high thoughts are
ever striving: they are not happy to
remain in the same place.
Like swans that leave their lake and
rise into the air, they leave their
home for a higher home.

April 22

**Small views are irresolute,
the more in haste,
the tardier they go.**

April 23

The man who controls his senses as a good driver controls his horses, and who is free from lower passions and pride, is admired even by the gods.

April 24

In being 'not two', all is the
same, all that is comprehended
in it; the wise in the ten
quarters, they all enter into
this Absolute Reason.

April 25

He is calm like the earth that
endures; he is steady like a column
that is firm; he is pure like a lake
that is clear; he is free from samsara,
the ever-returning life-in-death.

April 26

Better than a thousand useless
words is one word that gives peace.

April 27

Obey the nature of things,
and you are in concord with
The Way, calm and easy and
free from annoyance.

April 28

In the light of his vision he has found his freedom: his thoughts are peace and his work is peace.

April 29

When Mind and each
believing mind are not divided,
and undivided are each
believing mind and Mind,
this is where words fail;
for it is not of the past,
present or future.

April 30

If a man should conquer in battle a
thousand and thousand more, and
another should conquer himself,
his would be the greater victory,
because the greatest of victories is
the victory over oneself.

May

DAILY REFLECTIONS

May 1

Stopping of becoming is nirvana.

May 2

The body is a castle made of bones covered with flesh and blood. Pride and deceit, decay and death dwell within.

May 3

Whoever should intentionally
deprive a breathing thing of life,
there is an offence of expiation.

May 4

Wonderful, profound, illustrious,
hard art Thou to recognize.
Like a mock show Thou art seen,
and yet Thou art not seen at all.

May 5

'He insulted me, he hurt me,
he defeated me, he robbed me.'
Those who think such things
will not be free from hate.

May 6

Dispel thou doubt in me,
incline thy heart!
Full rare and seldom or
the wakened seen.
Of those rare men seen
seldom in the world,
lo, I am one,
physician without peer.

May 7

Pursue not the outer entanglements,
dwell not on the Inner Void;
be serene in the oneness of things,
and dualism vanishes by itself.

May 8

Through perseverance, vigilance and self-restraint, a wise person creates a safe harbour for herself that no storm can overwhelm.

May 9

As from a large heap of flowers
many garlands and wreaths are
made, so by a mortal in this
life there is much good
work to be done.

May 10

The wise one does not judge others,
not their words or deeds or what
they have or have not done.
The wise one only contemplates her
own words and deeds.

May 11

How long is the night to the
watchman; how long is the road
to the weary; how long is the
wandering of lives ending in death
for the fool who cannot
find the path!

May 12

When we return to the root,
we gain the meaning; when we
pursue external objects we
lose the reason.

May 13

Those who think the unreal is, and
the Real is not, they shall never
reach the Truth, lost in the path
of wrong thought.

May 14

If an eye never falls asleep,
all dreams will by themselves cease.

May 15

To try and understand one's inner
mind still chained to hopes and fears
– that prolongs the bondage.

May 16

My age is now full ripe; my life
draws to a close,
I leave you, I depart; the Self I've
made my refuge.

May 17

Who makes unbounded
love to become,
mindful, he sees the
attachments all destroyed.

May 18

If during the whole of life a fool
lives with a wise man, he never
knows the path of wisdom as
the spoon never knows the
taste of soup.

May 19

Deeds done in harmony with one's
path of life are those which bring
clarity and peace and harmony
to the doer.

May 20

Those who make channels for water control the water; makers of arrows make the arrows straight; carpenters control their timber; and the wise control their own minds.

May 21

In whatever person malice is
engendered, in that person love
should be made to become,
also compassion, also balance.

May 22

Whoever offers sacrifice, or whoever
gets others to do so – all these are
following a course of
merit benefiting many others.

May 23

Whosoever honours in reverence
those who are old in virtue and
holiness, he indeed conquers four
treasures: long life and health,
and power and joy.

May 24

There is an unborn, un-become,
unmade, incomposite, and were
there not, there would be no escape
from the born, the become, the
made and the composite world.

May 25

Better than a hundred years
lived in ignorance, without
contemplation, is one single day
of life lived in wisdom and deep
contemplation.

May 26

Better than a hundred years lived
in idleness and in weakness is a
single day of life lived with courage
and powerful striving.

May 27

Watchfulness is the path of
immortality: unwatchfulness is the
path of death. Those who are
watchful never die: those who do
not watch are already dead.

May 28

The fool who does evil to a man
who is good, to a man who is pure
and free from sin, the evil returns
to him like dust thrown
against the wind.

May 29

As a solid rock is indifferent to the wind and rain, so the wise are indifferent to criticism and praise.

May 30

A man may find pleasure in evil as
long as his evil has not given fruit;
but when the fruit of evil comes
then that man finds evil indeed.

May 31

Churning and churning water,
does not produce butter.

June

DAILY REFLECTIONS

June 1

Abandon the ways of confusion and
darkness and live in the light of
peace and harmony.

June 2

Have fire like a noble horse touched
by the whip. By faith, by virtue, by
wisdom and by right action, you
shall overcome the sorrows of life.

June 3

The moment we are enlightened within,
we go beyond the voidness of
a world confronting us.

June 4

Hold not a sin of little worth,
thinking 'this is little to me'.
The falling of drops of water will in
time fill a water-jar. Even so the
foolish man becomes full of evil
although he gather it little by little.

June 5

Unshakeable is freedom for me,
this is my last birth, there is now
not becoming again.

June 6

Who longs for the Great Self – he should pay homage to true dharma.

June 7

All beings fear before danger, life is dear to all. When a man considers this, he does not kill or cause to kill.

June 8

Stirred up for me shall unsluggish
energy become, called up unmuddled
mindfulness; calm and serene my
body, not turbulent; concentrated my
mind and one-pointed.

June 9

I have gone round in vain
the cycles of many lives, ever
striving to find the builder of the
house of life that must die! But now
I have seen thee, house builder:
never more shalt thou build this
house. The rafters of sin are broken,
the ridge-pole of ignorance is
destroyed. The fever of craving is
past: for my mortal mind is gone to
the joy of nirvana.

June 10

To aim at lasting achievements
whilst still exposed to this
world's distractions – that prolongs
the bondage.

June 11

So impermanent are the constructions, so transient, so unreliable.

June 12

If a man tries not to learn
he grows old just like an ox!
His body indeed grows old,
but his wisdom does not grow.

June 13

Nirvana is not of the nature of falsehood.

June 14

Anyone in whom passion is abandoned, in whom delusion is abandoned, is called one not bound by death.

June 15

O let us live in joy,
in love amongst those who hate!
Among men who hate,
let us live in love.

June 16

Who passion for all pleasure ends,
helped by the state of man-of-naught,
rid of all else, is yondermost release of
all sense released, he would
stay poised untrammelled
in that state.

June 17

O let us live in joy, although
having nothing! In joy let us live like
spirits of light!

June 18

Not to be helpful to others,
not to give to those in need,
this is the fruit of samsara.
Better than this is to renounce the
idea of self.

June 19

Only a man himself can be
master of himself: who else outside
could be his master?
When the Master and servant are
one, then there is true help and
self possession.

June 20

Any wrong or evil a man does is born in himself and is caused by himself; and this crushes the foolish man as a hard stone grinds the weaker stone.

June 21

If one find a friend
with whom to fare,
rapt in the well-abiding apt,
surmounting dangers one and all
with joy fare with him mindfully.

June 22

Here in the cool shade
of a santal tree
I dwell in solitude and silence,
in trance I meditate, from
all distractions far removed.

June 23

And the evil that grows in a man
is like a maluva creeper which
entangles the sal tree and the man is
brought down to that condition in
which his own enemy would wish
him to be.

June 24

O let us live in joy, in peace amongst
those who struggle!
Among men who struggle, let us live
in peace.

June 25

If you can be in silent quietness like
a broken gong that is silent, you
have reached the peace of nirvana
and your anger is peace.

June 26

We beg from you the good dharma
freeing us from suffering.
We beg the light dispelling
all our ignorance.
We beg from you the dharma – the
cure of all defilements.

June 27

Those who in their youth did not
live in self-harmony, and who did
not gain the true treasures of life,
are like long-legged old herons
standing by a lake without fish.

June 28

Through stillness joined
to insight true,
his passions are annihilated.
Stillness must first of all be found,
that springs from disregarding
worldly satisfactions.

June 29

Form should be seen as a mass of
foam, because easily crushed;
feeling as a water bubble, because
pleasurable only for a moment;
perception as a mirage,
because delusive.

June 30

How can there be laughter, how can there be pleasure, when the whole world is burning?
When you are in deep darkness, will you not ask for a lamp?

July

DAILY REFLECTIONS

July 1

The presence always of Mara,
the Lord of Death – do you
understand that?
Even the rich man when he is laid
low, departs alone – do you
understand that?

July 2

With passion gone and hate expelled,
let him in boundless measure then
quicken a heart of love,
every day and night zeal suffuse
all quarters to infinitude.

July 3

All the immaculate perfections
at all times encircle Thee,
as the stars surround the crescent,
O Thou blameless holy one.

July 4

Even as a great rock is not
shaken by the wind, the wise man is
not shaken by praise or blame.

July 5

He who for himself or others craves
not for sons or power or wealth, who
puts not his own success before
the success of righteousness,
he is virtuous, and righteous and wise.

July 6

To hope for miraculous blessings
and still have wrong opinions –
that prolongs the bondage.

July 7

If a man does something wrong,
let him not do it again and again.
Let him find no pleasure in his sin.
Painful is the accumulation
of wrongdoings.

July 8

If a man do something good, let him do it again and again. Let him find joy in his good work. Joyful is the accumulation of good work.

July 9

A man may find pain in doing good as long as his good has not given fruit; but when the fruit of good comes then that man finds good indeed.

July 10

Here, from within my heart,
I make the vow
to shun all evil – to achieve the good.
From deep within my heart
I seek my refuge.

July 11

Then you forfeit the truth of the real; your fallen condition shocks you no longer. Burning with grief you yearn for re-union with him whom you cherish.

July 12

Palaces built of earth and stone and wood,
wealthy men endowed with food
and dress and finery,
legions of retainers who throng
round the mighty –
these are like castles in the air,
like rainbows in the sky,
and how deluded those who think
of this as truth.

July 13

Our thoughts provoked by
diverse apparition –
all are like flowers in autumn, clouds
across the sky,
how deluded assembled birds if you
have thought of them as permanent.

July 14

For he whose mind is well
trained in the ways that lead to
light, who surrenders the bondage of
attachments and finds joy in his
freedom from bondage, who free
from the darkness of passions shines
pure in radiance of light, even in
this mortal life, he enjoys the
immortal nirvana.

July 15

He who is pleasure-quit, as
conqueror fares,
hath found and known the end of
birth-and-death.
Cool man, cool as the waters
of the lake.

July 16

All creatures, all breathers,
all beings and everything –
may they all find good fortune,
may none come to harm.

July 17

Material shape is bereft of
three things –
life, heat and consciousness –
see that it is thrown aside.
When the body is cast off
discarded there it lies, food for
others, senseless.

July 18

Make haste and do what is good;
keep your mind away from evil. If a
man is slow in doing good, his mind
finds pleasure in evil.

July 19

Here the disciple dwells suffusing
one direction of space with a heart
linked to friendliness, then a second,
then a third, then a fourth, then
above, then below, around,
and everywhere.

July 20

And so he dwells recognizing himself in all, suffusing the entire world with a heart linked to friendliness, far-reaching, widespread, free, unlimited, free from enmity and malice.

July 21

One who values happiness for himself but creates anxiety for others is confused.

July 22

The man who has no evil
cannot be hurt by evil.

July 23

Dharma is truth, restraint is
Brahma-faring,
The Middle Way pursuing, brahman,
the way to Brahma-attainment.
Due honour pay thou to the
upright-minded,
who so doth this, him do
I call Tide-rider.

July 24

So long as monks become full of faith, growth may be expected for monks, not decline. So long as monks become conscientious, become afraid of blame, become great listeners, become of stirred-up energy, become mindful, become wise, growth may be expected from monks, not decline.

July 25

Even as rain breaks through an ill-thatched house, passions will break through an ill-guarded mind.

July 26

Gone greed, gone guile,
gone thirst, gone grudge,
and winnowed all delusions, faults,
wantless in all the world become.

July 27

Good friends at one time,
of a sudden they dislike you.
You try to please them,
quite in vain – the worldly are
not easily contented.

July 28

Of his betters he is envious, with his
equals there is strife;
to inferiors he is haughty, mad for
praise and wroth at blame;
is there ever any goodness in these
foolish men?

July 29

He who lives only for pleasures, and
whose soul is not in harmony, who
considers not the food he eats, is idle
and has not the power of virtue –
such a man is moved by Mara, is
moved by selfish temptations, even
as a weak tree is shaken by the wind.

July 30

Let him be strenuous, upright and
truly straight, without conceit of
self, easily contented and joyous,
free of cares; let him not be
submerged by things of this world;
let him not take upon the burden of
worldly goods; let his senses be
controlled; let him be wise, not
puffed up and let him not desire
great possessions even for his family.
Let him do nothing that is mean or
that the wise would reprove.

July 31

Self-applause, belittling others,
or encouragement to sin,
some such evil's sure to happen
where one fool meets another.

August

DAILY REFLECTIONS

August 1

The fools are no one's friends, so
have the Buddhas taught us;
they cannot love unless their interest
in themselves impels them.

August 2

And death, the end of all, makes
an end of man who, ever thirsty
for desires, gathers the flowers of
sensuous passions.

August 3

Consciousness is unending.

August 4

Both fuel and air must be present
for a fire to blaze up; so the fire of
passions is born from a combination of
a sense object with the imaginations.

August 5

Think not of the faults of others,
of what they have done or not done.
Think rather of your own sins,
of the things you have done
or not done.

August 6

He hears dharma and learns it by
heart, examines the import of things
so learnt and is in an ecstasy of
delight over them; strong desire rises
in him; he is emboldened; he weighs
it all; he strives; being self-resolute,
by means of body, he realizes the
highest truth itself.

August 7

Who, unless he be quite mad,
would make plans which do reckon
with death, when he sees the world
so unsubstantial and frail, like a
water bubble?

August 8

Even as on a heap of rubbish thrown away by the side of the road, a lotus flower may grow and blossom with its pure perfume giving joy to the soul, in the same way among the blind multitudes shines pure the light of wisdom of the student who follows the Buddha, the One who is truly awake.

August 9

What is clinging? There are four
kinds of clinging: Clinging to
pleasure. Clinging to views.
Clinging to rules, techniques and
vows. Clinging to self.

August 10

And from all other cares
released, the mind set on
collecting my own spirit,
to unify and discipline my
spirit I will strive.

August 11

Invisible and subtle is the mind, and
it flies after fancies wherever it likes:
but let the wise man guard well his
mind, for a mind well guarded is a
source of great joy.

August 12

Neither in the sky, nor in the deep in the ocean, nor in a mountain-cave, nor anywhere, can a man be free from the evil he has done.

August 13

A man who has imposed strict
mindfulness on all he does,
and remains as watchful as a
gatekeeper at a city-gate, is safe from
injury by the passions, just as a well
guarded town is safe from its foes.

August 14

The glorious chariots of kings wear
out, and the body wears out and
grows old; but the virtue of the
good never grows old, and thus they
can teach the good to those
who are good.

August 15

When a man considers the world as a bubble of froth, and as the illusion of an appearance, then the king of death has no power over him.

August 16

The instructed disciple disregards
material shapes and the rest; by
disregarding he is passionless;
through passionlessness he is freed;
in freedom, the knowledge comes to
be – I am freed – and he has
foreknowledge: Destroyed is birth,
lived is the Brahma-faring, done is
what was done, there is nothing
more of being such or such.

August 17

Grasping after systems,
imprisoned by dogmas for the most
part is this world. But he who does
not go in for system-grasping he
neither doubts nor is perplexed; by
not depending on others, knowledge
herein comes to be his own.

August 18

Train yourself in this way:
from higher to higher, from strength
to strength we will strive,
and we will come to realize
unsurpassed freedom.

August 19

A wrong action may not
bring its reaction at once, even as
fresh milk turns not sour at once:
like a smoldering fire concealed
under ashes it consumes the
wrongdoer, the fool.

August 20

He who in early days was unwise
but later found wisdom, he sheds
light over the world like that of the
moon when free from clouds.

August 21

I am the result of my own deeds,
heir to deeds. Whatever deed I do,
whether good or evil, I shall become
its heir. This should be
contemplated often.

August 22

Mastery of the world is achieved by
mastery of the pure Self.

August 23

By what earthly path could you entice the Buddha who, enjoying all, can wander through the pathless ways of the Infinite – the Buddha who is awake, whose victory cannot be turned into defeat, and whom no one can conquer?

August 24

Stirred for me shall be unsluggish energy, called up unmuddled mindfulness; calmed and serene my body, not turbulent; concentrated my mind and one-pointed.

August 25

Who crushes the great 'I am' conceit
finds indeed happiness supreme.

August 26

Abandon what is wrong.
It is possible to abandon it. Were it
not possible to abandon what is
wrong, I would not say: Abandon it.
But because it is possible, therefore I
say: Abandon what is wrong.

August 27

Live not a low life; remember and
forget not; follow not wrong ideas;
sink not into the world.

August 28

They in the world are 'Brahmans'
who are unfettered and awake.

August 29

Swan follow the path of the sun by
the miracle of flying through air.
Men who are strong conquer evil
and its armies; and then rise far
above the world.

August 30

Sense pleasures are impermanent. The search for them involves suffering, and they are enjoyed in constant disquiet; their loss leads to much grief, and their gain can never result in lasting satisfaction.

August 31

Abandoning what is unwholesome, you ought to ponder what is wholesome, for that will bring you advantages in this world and help you to win the heighest goal.

September

September 1

Better than power over all the earth,
better than going to heaven and
better than dominion over the
worlds is the joy of the man who
enters the river of life that leads
to nirvana.

September 2

Brahma-faring is lived for the goal of restraint, for the goal of abandoning, for the goal of dispassion, for the goal of making to cease.

September 3

The merit that is due to going forth benefits many people.

September 4

When desires go, joy comes.
The follower of Buddha finds this truth.

September 5

Drench, pervade, fill and pervade
this body itself with zest and ease
that are born of contemplation.

September 6

Not to hurt by deeds of words,
self-control as taught in the Rules,
moderation in food, the solitude of
one's room and one's bed, and
the practice of the highest
consciousness: this is the teachings
of the Buddhas who are awake.

September 7

If ill-will or the desire to hurt others
should stir your mind, purify it with
the opposite. Friendliness and
compassion are their antidotes; for
they are as ever as opposed to hatred
as light to darkness.

September 8

I say it is by destroying, stilling, stopping, renouncing and abandoning all imaginings, all supposings, all thoughts of, 'I am the doer,' 'Mine is the doer,' all latent 'I am,' and the Truth-finder is freed.

September 9

As an axle of a chariot must be
lubricated so that it may run
properly, so the wise man employs
food only to maintain his life.

September 10

Victory brings hate, because the
defeated man is unhappy.
He who surrenders victory and
defeat, this man finds joy.

September 11

The fair tree of Void abounds
with flowers,
acts of compassion of
many kinds,
and fruit for others
appearing spontaneously,
for this joy has no actual
thought of another.

September 12

A man whose words are lies, who transgresses the Great Law, and who scorns the higher world – there is no evil this man may not do.

September 13

The fair tree of thought that
knows no duality,
spreads through the triple world.
It bears the flower and fruit
of compassion, and its name is
service of others.

September 14

It is better to spend one day contemplating the birth and death of all things than a hundred years never contemplating beginnings and endings.

September 15

See thought as thought, O fool,
and leave all false views.
Gain purification in bliss supreme,
for here lies final perfection.

September 16

He who has no craving desires,
either for this world or for another
world, who free from desires is
in infinite freedom – him call
I a Brahmin.

September 17

Even as the moon makes light
in black darkness,
even so in one moment the supreme
bliss removes all defilements.

September 18

By oneself the evil is done and it is oneself that suffers: by oneself the evil is not done, and by one's Self one becomes pure.

September 19

As in nirvana, so in samsara.
Do not think there is any distinction.
Yet it possesses no single nature
for I know it as quite pure.

September 20

He who does what should not be done, who forgets the true aim of life and sinks into transient pleasures – he will one day envy the man who lives in high contemplation.

September 21

'This is myself and this is another.'
Be free of this bond which
encompasses you about,
and your own self is
thereby released.

September 22

From passion arises sorrow and from passion arises fear. If a man is free from passion, he is free from fear and sorrow.

September 23

He who goes for refuge to Buddha,
to Truth and to those whom he
taught, he goes indeed to a great
refuge. Then he sees the
four great truths.

September 24

Do not err in this matter of
self and other.
Everything is Buddha
without exception.
Here is that immaculate
final stage,
where thought is pure in
its true nature.

September 25

Neither him given to laxity,
nor him of little strength,
may reach nirvana,
the freedom of all ill.

September 26

There are four kinds of grasping: grasping after sense-pleasures, grasping after opinion, grasping after rule and rite, grasping after the theory of 'self'.

September 27

There are six groups of craving: craving for material shapes, craving for things heard, smelt, tasted, touched, craving for states of mind.

September 28

To strive for purity of vision, and yet
be blinded by faulty judgement –
that prolongs the bondage.

September 29

This uprising by way of cause is profound and has the appearance of being profound. It is not knowing, not discovering, not penetrating this dharma that this generation, having become entangled like a ball of string, and covered with blight like coarse grass and rushes, cannot pass over the Waste, the Bad Bourn, the Downfall, the Faring-on.

September 30

When a man knows the solitude of
silence, and feels the joy of
quietness, he is then free from fear
and he feels the joy of the dharma.

October

DAILY REFLECTIONS

October 1

**One in All,
All in One –
if only this is realized,
no more worry about you
not being perfect.**

October 2

Material shape is not yours,
nor are feeling, perception,
the constructions or consciousness.
These are not yours. Put them away.

October 3

Not even the gods can turn the victory of conquering oneself into defeat.

October 4

Few cross the river of time and are
able to reach nirvana.
Most of them run up and down only
on this side of the river.

October 5

When a fool does evil work, he forgets that he is lighting a fire wherein he must burn one day.

October 6

As rain penetrates an improperly
shingled roof,
so passion overwhelms a confused
mind.

October 7

The perfect way knows no difficulties
except it refuses to make preferences.

October 8

He who like the moon is pure,
bright, clear and serene; whose
pleasure for things that pass away –
him I call a Brahmin.

October 9

Who, being rich, supports
not their parents in their age,
when gone is all their youth;
and he who parents strikes,
doth brother vex with words,
wife's mother, sister too;
know him as outcast vile.

October 10

All beings and everything –
may they all see luck,
may none come to evil.

October 11

A lake is dharma, with virtue's
strand for bathing,
clear, undefiled, praised by the good
to good men,
wherein truth masters of law
come bathing,
so, clean of limb, to the Beyond
cross over.

October 12

He who is free from the
bondage of men and from the
bondage of the gods: who is free
of all things in creation –
him I call a Brahmin.

October 13

Even the most frightful gales could not possibly shake trees that have never been planted.

October 14

Who can trace the invisible path of the man who soars in the sky of liberation, the infinite Void without beginning, whose passions are peace, and over whom pleasure has no power? His path is as difficult to trace as that of the birds of the air.

October 15

He who is powerful, noble, who lives a life of inner heroism, the all-seer, the all-conqueror, the ever-pure, who has reached the end of his journey, who like the Buddha is awake – him I call a Brahmin.

October 16

A recluse's goal is patience and forbearance. Wisdom is his ambition, moral habit is his resolve, nothingness his want, nirvana is his fulfilment.

October 17

Since they have compassion for him,
as a mother for her child,
a man, through the gods'
compassion, sees good
everywhere.

October 18

When beyond meditation and
contemplation a Brahmin has
reached the far shore, then he
obtains the supreme vision and all
his fetters are broken.

October 19

Wherever the sage dwells, be it in village, forest, mountain or valley, there the peace and harmony are always increased.

October 20

By day the sun shines, and by night shines the moon. The warrior shines in his armour, and the Brahmin in his meditation. But the Buddha shines by day and by night – in the brightness of his glory shines the man who is awake.

October 21

Ask not of birth but of
the faring ask!
From wood is awe-
inspiring fire begot:
from lowly clan noble
becomes the sage
who is steadfast and by
modesty restrained.

October 22

There are four bases of sympathy: charity, kind speech, doing a good turn and treating all alike.

October 23

Consumed by wisdom, faults cease to thrive and grow, like a tree which flares up after it has been struck by a thunderbolt.

October 24

Conquest engenders; the conquered lives in misery. But who so is at peace and passionless, happily doth he live; conquest has he abandoned and defeat.

October 25

He who speaks words that
are peaceful and useful and true,
words that offend no one –
him I call a Brahmin.

October 26

By entering on the eightfold path, which has morality, concentration and wisdom as its three divisions, and which is holy, incorruptible and straight, one forsakes those faults which are the cause of suffering and one attains the state of absolute peace.

October 27

This is the beginning of the life of
the wise monk; self-control
of the senses, happiness,
living under moral law, and whose
life is pure and who are ever striving.

October 28

He whose vision is deep, who is wise, who knows the path and what is outside the path, who has attained the highest end – him I call a Brahmin.

October 29

The conqueror gets one who
conquers him;
Th' abuser wins abuse,
thus by evolution of the deed
a man that spoils is spoiled
in his turn.

October 30

Let him no creatures kill
and none incite
to kill, nor sanction others
taking life,
but put by violence for
all that lives.

October 31

Arise! Rouse thyself by thy Self;
train thyself by thy Self,
and ever watchful, thou shalt
live in supreme joy.

November

DAILY REFLECTIONS

November 1

Mid men of pride, no man of
pride himself,
bond-overcomer who hath
no bonds left,
who understandeth ill,
its base and scope,
oblation-worthy is the
Man-thus-come.

November 2

He who in this world has gone
beyond good and evil and both,
who free from sorrows is free
from passions and is pure – him I
call a Brahmin.

November 3

Easy to see are others' faults,
those of self are hard to see.
Surely the faults of other men a man
doth winnow as 'twere chaff, but
those of the self he covers up like a
crafty gamester losing his throw.

November 4

Let no man endanger his duty, the good of his soul, for the good of another, however great. When he has seen the good of his soul, let him follow it with earnestness.

November 5

He goes on, having suffused the four quarters with a heart possessed of love, of compassion, of joy, of balance, above, below, across, everywhere, he goes on with a heart that is wide-spreading, vast, boundless, without enmity or malice.

November 6

All material shapes, feelings,
perceptions, constructions, and all
consciousness, whether past, future
or present, subjective or objective,
gross or subtle, mean or excellent,
near or far, must all be seen as:
this is not mine, I am not this,
this is not myself.

November 7

He who in his vision is free from
doubts and, having all, longs for
nothing, for he has reached
immortal freedom –
him call I a Brahmin.

November 8

If acts of thought are done through love
towards his fellows in the Brahma-faring,
both openly and in private – this is a
matter which conduces to unity.

November 9

Let him first find what is right and then he can teach it to others, thus avoiding useless pain.

November 10

He who hath razed all harbours of the
mind, in whom abides no claim to
things whate'er, he, unattached to
things of here or hence, oblation-
worthy is the Man-thus-come.

November 11

There is not in the world an evil
deed that lies hidden. The Self, O
man, knows what of you is true or
false. Ah, sir, the lovely Self you
despise who in the small self hides
the self that is evil.

November 12

Faith is the wealth here best for man;
dharma pursued brings happiness;
and truth is sweet beyond compare;
life wisely lived they say is best.

November 13

By faith the flood is crossed;
by earnestness the sea;
by vigour ill is passed;
by wisdom he is cleansed.

November 14

Freedom of heart that is love will
be made actual by us, made much
of, made a vehicle, made a basis,
exercised, augmented and
thoroughly set going.

November 15

Ten qualities are required of those
who tread the eightfold path:
steadfastness, sincerity, self-respect,
vigilance, seclusion from the world,
contentment with little, simplicity of
tastes, non-attachment, aversion of
worldly activity and patience.

November 16

Abandoning the taking of what is not given, abstaining from it, the recluse Gautama lives as one who takes only what is given, who waits for it to be given; not by stealing he lives with Self become pure.

November 17

This contemplation is peaceful and excellent. It is for gaining tranquillity, for reaching one-pointed concentration. This knowledge is not in order to develop the habit of painful self denial.

November 18

You would like to possess something
that was permanent, stable, eternal,
not liable to change, that would
stand fast like unto the eternal.
But can you see such a possession?
Neither can I.

November 19

Lo! Like a fragrant lotus
at the dawn
of day, full blown, with virgin
wealth of scent.
Behold the Buddha's glory
shining forth,
as in the vaulted heaven beams
the sun!

November 20

Who has bad men as friends,
nor makes friends with good,
who chooses men's bad ways:
a source of suffering that.

November 21

Who fitly acts and toils
and strives shall riches find;
by trust shall fame acquire;
by giving, friends shall bind.

November 22

There are four bases of sympathy.
What four?
Charity, kind speech, doing good
and treating all alike.

November 23

And lovers of the home
who hold in faith these four,
truth, dharma, firmness, gift,
hence gone shall grieve
no more.

November 24

Plain is the weal in life,
plain is the suffering:
prospers who dharma loves,
suffers who dharma hates.

November 25

He who has virtue and vision, who follows dharma, the Path of Perfection, whose words are truth, and does the work to be done – the world loves such a man.

November 26

You must slay anger if you
would live happily.
You must slay anger, if you
would weep no more.

November 27

Whatever wholesome dharmas there may be, they are all headed by concentration, they bend towards concentration, lead to concentration, incline to concentration.

November 28

He who has reached the yon
and nigh of things,
so all are ended, quenched
and no more,
calm man, and in attachment's
end released,
oblation-worthy is the
Man-thus-come.

November 29

He is not seen to come,
nor known to stay or go;
as signless and motionless the
supreme Lord is known.

November 30

One who can recite many sacred
verses but cannot live by them is like
an accountant who tallies the wealth
of others. He does not live in peace
and harmony.

December

DAILY REFLECTIONS

December 1

Here Sun and Moon lose their distinction,
in her the triple world is formed.
O know this yogini, the perfecter of
thought and unity of the Innate.

December 2

Seer of the end and term of
bond and birth,
who passion's ways hath wholly
left behind,
the cleansed, spotless, taintless,
without flaw,
oblation-worthy is the
Man-thus-come.

December 3

The one steadfast, released from
views is unsullied by the world,
not blamed by Self.

December 4

The mind is the sea for a man; its data are made of mental states. Whoever overcomes its data...is called one who has crossed the sea of mind with its waves, its whirlpools, with its sharks, its demons – crossed over, gone beyond, the brahman stands on dry land.

December 5

There is no fire like lust, and no chains like those of hate. There is no net like illusion and no rushing torrent like desire.

December 6

Regarding body as body, feelings
as feelings, thoughts as thoughts,
mental states as mental states,
control the hankering and dejection
in this world.

December 7

Regard the world as void; an e'er
alert, uproot false view of self.
Thus Mogharaja, thou wouldst be
Death's crosser; and regarding thus
the world, Death's king doth
see thee not.

December 8

Not to consider 'I am this,' that is freedom.

December 9

In freedom I am freed.

December 10

Seeing in what's impermanent the permanent, in what is ill what's well, in what is not-Self the Self, in what is ugly beauty, these are the erroneous views of the scatter-brained and unintelligent... They tread the round of becoming; theirs is the road of birth and death.

December 11

He is happy in his solitude who glad at heart has dharma learnt and the vision sees! Happy is that kindness towards the world; on no creature works harm.

December 12

Men expert in the result of deeds.
The world revolves by deeds,
mankind revolves by deeds:
as pin holds fast the rolling chariot's
wheel, so beings in bondage are
held by deeds.

December 13

And they who praise the
blameworthy,
and they who blame the
praiseworthy,
cull with the mouth the
seeds of woe,
not from the seeds raise happiness.

December 14

Just as the dawn is the forerunner,
the harbinger of the sun's arising,
even so is friendship with the lovely
the forerunner, the harbinger of the
arising of the seven limbs of
wisdom.

December 15

This that is called thought and mind and consciousness, this by day and night dissolves as one thing and reappears as another. As a monkey passing through the jungle catches hold of a bough and having let it go, takes hold of another, even so that which is called thought and mind and consciousness, this by night and day dissolves as one thing and reappears as another.

December 16

A man is not called wise because he
talks and talks again; but if he is
peaceful, loving and fearless then he
is in truth called wise.

December 17

Creatures are heirs to their deeds.

December 18

Do not trivialize small acts of peace and harmony, thinking, 'I will never reap what I have sown'.

A pitcher is filled one drop of water at a time and a person centred in oneness who proceeds in peace and harmony will soon manifest the peace and harmony in his life.

December 19

If one abandons onslaught on creatures, abstains from it, lays aside stick, lays aside knife, he lives modest, merciful, compassionate towards all living creatures. He is not crooked in body, speech, thought.

December 20

He who destroys life, who utters
lies, who takes what is not given to
him, who goes to the wife of
another, who gets drunk with strong
drinks – he digs up the very roots
of his life.

December 21

Not to be reached by locomotion is
World's End ever:
yet there is no release from ill till it
has been reached.
So let a man become a World-
knower, World-ender,
let him have led the Brahma-faring –
knowing World's End,
as one pacified,
he longs not for this
or another world.

December 22

Go along having Self as lamp, Self as refuge and none other as refuge; having dharma as lamp, dharma as refuge and none other as refuge.

December 23

Formerly also, as well as now, all material shape was impermanent, suffering, liable to change. By right wisdom, seeing it thus as it really comes to be, sorrow, grief, lamentation and despair wane.

December 24

A man is not a follower of righteousness because he talks much learned talk; but although a man be not learned, if he forgets not the right path, if his work is rightly done, then he is a follower of righteousness.

December 25

A man is not a great man because
he is a warrior and kills other men;
but because he hurts not any living
being, he in truth is called
great man.

December 26

Material shape is like a ball of foam,
feelings like unto a bubble blown,
perceptions like a mirage are,
the constructions like a
plantain tree,
consciousness like an illusion:
so said the Kinsman of the Sun.

December 27

And what is right speech? Abstaining from lying, from divisive speech, from abusive speech, and from idle chatter: this is called right speech.

December 28

He should desire to pursue neither
extremes,
committing nothing that the Self
would blame.

December 29

Devas and Truth-seekers see the fool
walking unevenly in the world;
wherefore let the 'master of himself'
walk recollectedly, heedfully,
contemplative.

December 30

The self is not in Self.

December 31

The end remains untold.